Every Kid's Guide to
Handling Feelings

Written by
JOY BERRY

GROLIER ENTERPRISES INC.
Danbury, Connecticut

About the Author and Publisher

Joy Berry's mission in life is to help families cope with everyday problems and to help children become competent, responsible, happy individuals. To achieve her goal, she has written over two hundred self-help books for children from birth through age twelve. Her work revolutionized children's publishing by providing families with practical, how-to, living skills information that was previously unavailable in children's books.

Joy gathered a dedicated team of experts, including psychologists, educators, child developmentalists, writers, editors, designers, and artists, to form her publishing company and to help produce her work.

The company, Living Skills Press, produces thoroughly researched books and audio-visual materials that successfully combine humor and education to teach subjects ranging from how to clean a bedroom to how to resolve problems and get along with other people.

Managing Editor: Ellen Klarberg
Copy Editor: Kate Dickey
Contributing Editors: Libby Byers, Nancy Cochran, Maureen Dryden,
Yona Flemming, Kathleen Mohr, Susan Motycka
Editorial Assistant: Sandy Passarino

Art Director: Laurie Westdahl
Design: Abigail Johnston, Laurie Westdahl
Production: Abigail Johnston, Caroline Rennard
Illustrations designed by: Bartholomew
Inker: Susie Hornig
Colorer: Tuan Pham
Composition: Curt Chelin

Grolier Enterprises Inc. offers a varied selection of children's book racks and tote bags.
For details on ordering, please write:
Grolier Enterprises Inc., Sherman Turnpike, Danbury, CT 06816 Attn: Premium Department

Feelings can have a positive or negative influence on your life depending on how you handle them.

EVERY KID'S GUIDE TO HANDLING FEELINGS can help you handle your feelings in acceptable ways by teaching you the following:

- what feelings are,
- what common comfortable feelings are,
- what common uncomfortable feelings are, and
- what the four steps are for handling uncomfortable feelings.

Every person experiences emotions.
Another word for emotions is *feelings.*
There are two kinds of feelings. There are
comfortable feelings and *uncomfortable* feelings.

Comfortable feelings make people feel good.

Uncomfortable feelings make people feel bad.

Comfortable feelings can help you have fun and enjoy life.

Love is a comfortable feeling.

Love is feeling that other people care about you. It is feeling that others value you.

Acceptance is another comfortable feeling.

Acceptance is feeling that other people like and respect you.

Security is a comfortable feeling.

Security is feeling that you are safe.

Pride is another comfortable feeling.

Pride is feeling good about yourself and the things you do.

Confidence is a comfortable feeling.

Confidence is feeling that you can do things on your own.

Happiness is another comfortable feeling.

Happiness is feeling joyful and contented.

Uncomfortable feelings can make you feel bad.
Even so, uncomfortable feelings can be helpful.

Uncomfortable feelings can make you want to do what needs to be done.

Uncomfortable feelings can help you grow and change for the better.

Uncomfortable feelings can help you notice and appreciate your comfortable feelings.

Fear is an uncomfortable feeling. Fear is feeling frightened or scared. You might
- be afraid of things you don't understand,
- be afraid of things you think could hurt you,
- want to get away from things that scare you, or
- want to be with someone when you are afraid.

When you are afraid, don't pretend to be big
and brave because of what people might think if you
are not.

It is best if you
- admit you are afraid,
- pay attention to your fears,
- realize your fear might be warning you that you
  are in danger,
- be cautious,
- tell someone else about your fear, and
- find out all you can about the things that frighten
  you.

Anxiety is another uncomfortable feeling. Anxiety is feeling tense, worried, or nervous. When you are anxious, you might

- worry that something could hurt you,
- worry that someone will get angry with you,
- worry about things you do not understand, or
- worry that you will make a mistake or have an accident.

When you are anxious, try not to
- pretend that you are not anxious or
- hide your true feelings.

It is best if you
- admit you are anxious,
- talk to someone about your worries, and
- find out everything you can about whatever is worrying you.

Frustration is an uncomfortable feeling. Frustration is feeling upset, irritated, and discouraged. When you are frustrated, you might want to express your frustration by crying, yelling, jumping up and down, or hitting things. It is OK to do these things as long as you do not bother other people or damage or destroy anything. This might mean you will need to go outside or into another room while you express your frustration.

When you are frustrated, try not to do anything that will

- hurt yourself,
- hurt others, or
- damage or destroy anyone's property.

It is best if you

- slow down,
- try again at another time, or
- ask someone to help you.

Defeat is another uncomfortable feeling. Defeat is feeling that you have lost or failed. It is feeling that you have been beaten. You might

- feel embarrassed about failing,
- not want others to know about your failures, or
- get discouraged and want to give up when you fail.

When you fail, try not to
- believe you are a loser,
- believe you will never win, or
- stop trying.

It is best if you
- remember that everyone loses once in a while,
- remember that no one wins all the time,
- work harder,
- practice more, and
- keep trying.

Humiliation is an uncomfortable feeling.
Humiliation is feeling embarrassed or foolish.
When you are humiliated, you might not want to
- be around the people who were there when
  you were humiliated or
- remember humiliating experiences.

When you are humiliated, try not to
- get back at the people who humiliated you or
- embarrass other people.

It is best if you
- ignore the humiliation and
- walk away.

Guilt is another uncomfortable feeling. Guilt is feeling that you have done something wrong. When you feel guilty, you might

- feel ashamed and embarrassed,
- not want anyone to know about what you did,
- find it difficult to admit you did something wrong, and
- find it difficult to say you are sorry.

When you feel guilty, try not to
- lie,
- pretend nothing happened,
- hide what you have done wrong, or
- spend a lot of time wishing you had acted differently.

It is best if you
- admit you did something wrong,
- say you are sorry, and
- try to make up for what you did.

Grief is an uncomfortable feeling. Grief is feeling sad. When you are sad, you might

- cry,
- want to be alone,
- wish that whatever makes you sad hadn't happened, or
- want to forget about what makes you sad.

When you are sad, try not to
- pretend that nothing is wrong or
- hide your grief.

It is best if you
- admit that you are sad and
- tell someone about your grief.

Disappointment is another uncomfortable feeling. Disappointment is feeling let down. When you are disappointed, you might

- cry,
- want to be alone,
- be angry with the people who disappoint you,
- wonder whether they will let you down again, or
- be afraid to trust them until you are shown they will not disappoint you again.

When you are disappointed, try not to
- say mean things or
- get back at the people who disappoint you.

It is best if you
- tell someone that you are disappointed,
- explain why you are disappointed, and
- find out why you were let down.

Rejection is an uncomfortable feeling. Rejection is feeling unwanted. It is feeling that you are not liked or accepted. When you are rejected, you might

- wonder about yourself and your abilities,
- want to avoid people who reject you, or
- want to prove to the people who reject you that you are OK.

When you feel rejected, try not to
- believe that you are no good or
- give up.

It is best if you
- keep trying,
- remember no one person is liked by everyone,
- remember no one person can be good at everything,
- think about your good qualities,
- do the things you do well,
- try to be with people who like and accept you, and
- try not to spend time with the people who do not appreciate you.

Loneliness is another uncomfortable feeling. Loneliness is feeling that you are all alone. When you are lonely, you might

- feel rejected,
- feel sad,
- be bored, or
- want someone to notice you.

When you are lonely, try not to
- think that no one wants to play with you or be your friend,
- refuse to make friends, or
- get someone to notice you by behaving badly.

It is best if you
- admit that you are lonely,
- find someone to play with, and
- make friends with someone.

Jealousy is an uncomfortable feeling. Jealousy is wishing you were like another person. It can also be wishing you had something another person has. It is normal for young people to
- be jealous of their brothers and sisters,
- want to be the best, and
- want to have more.

When you are jealous, try not to
- say mean things about other people,
- hurt other people in any way, or
- compete with other people.

It is best if you
- tell someone about your jealousy,
- ask for help or attention,
- try not to compare yourself with others,
- realize you are a special person and unlike anyone else,
- realize you have many things that no one else has, and
- remember you can do some things better than other people.

Anger is another uncomfortable feeling. Anger is feeling bad-tempered. You might want to express your anger by crying, yelling, jumping up and down, or hitting things. It is OK to do these things as long as you do not bother other people or damage or destroy anything. This might mean you will need to go outside or into another room while you express your anger.

When you feel angry, try not to do anything that will
- hurt yourself,
- hurt others, or
- damage or destroy anyone's property.

It is best if you
- tell someone you are angry,
- explain why you are angry, and
- try to do something about whatever is making you angry.

You need to handle uncomfortable feelings properly if they are going to help you. These four steps will assist you in handling your uncomfortable feelings:

Step 1. Face it.

Define the emotion you feel. Ask yourself, "What do I feel?"

Step 2. Accept it.

Try to understand why you feel the way you do.
Then realize that it is OK to feel the way you do.
Ask yourself, "Why do I feel this way?"

Step 3. Decide what to do.

Decide what you need to do to make yourself feel better. Ask yourself, "What should I do about my uncomfortable feeling?"

Do not do anything that will
- hurt yourself,
- hurt others, or
- damage or destroy anyone's property.

Step 4. Do it.

Do what you have decided to do.

Following these four steps is called *resolving your feelings.* It might not be easy to resolve your feelings by yourself. You might need help. Choose a person you trust and respect. Ask that person to help you.

Uncomfortable feelings can
- make you want to do what needs to be done,
- help you grow and change for the better, and
- help you notice and appreciate your comfortable feelings.

Comfortable feelings can help you have fun and enjoy life.

This is why it is important for you to have both comfortable and uncomfortable feelings.